Don't. Make. Tea.

Rob Drummond

T0021660

methuen | drama

LONDON • NEW YORK • OXFORD • NEW DELHI • SYDNEY

METHUEN DRAMA
Bloomsbury Publishing Plc
50 Bedford Square, London, WC1B 3DP, UK
1385 Broadway, New York, NY 10018, USA
29 Earlsfort Terrace, Dublin 2, Ireland

BLOOMSBURY, METHUEN DRAMA and the Methuen
Drama logo are trademarks of Bloomsbury Publishing Plc

First published in Great Britain 2024

Cover image by Andy Catlin

Cover artwork by Laura Whitehouse

Bloomsbury Publishing Plc does not have any control over, or responsibility
for, any third-party websites referred to or in this book. All internet addresses
given in this book were correct at the time of going to press. The author and
publisher regret any inconvenience caused if addresses have changed or sites
have ceased to exist, but can accept no responsibility for any such changes.

No rights in incidental music or songs contained in the work are hereby
granted and performance rights for any performance/presentation
whatsoever must be obtained from the respective copyright owners.

All rights whatsoever in this play are strictly reserved and application
for performance etc. should be made before rehearsals to Casarotto Ramsay
& Associates Ltd., 3rd Floor, 7 Savoy Court, Strand, London WC2R 0EX.
No performance may be given unless a licence has been obtained.

A catalogue record for this book is available from the British Library.

A catalog record for this book is available from the Library of Congress.

ISBN: PB: 978-1-3505-0191-1
ePDF: 978-1-3505-0192-8
eBook: 978-1-3505-0193-5

Series: Modern Plays

Typeset by Mark Heslington Ltd, Scarborough, North Yorkshire

To find out more about our authors and books visit
www.bloomsbury.com and sign up for our newsletters.

BIRDS OF PARADISE
THEATRE COMPANY

in association with Traverse Theatre present

Don't. Make. Tea.

Rob Drummond

Don't. Make. Tea. was first performed at the Traverse
Theatre, Edinburgh, on 5 October 2022, and returned
for a UK tour in March 2024.

ROB DRUMMOND

WRITER

Rob Drummond is a playwright, performer and director and an associate artist with the Traverse Theatre in Edinburgh. Rob's wide-ranging work includes two CATS award-winning plays for young audiences, *Mr Write* (National Theatre of Scotland) and *Uncanny Valley* (Borderline Theatre and Edinburgh International Science Festival), *Rob Drummond: Wrestling* (The Arches), for which Rob trained as a professional wrestler, *The Majority* (National Theatre); the multi-award-winning *Bullet Catch* (The Arches), CATS award-winning *Quiz Show* (The Traverse), acclaimed thriller *Grain in the Blood* (The Traverse), the first ever stage adaptation of beloved Scottish comic strip *The Broons* (Selladoor), and dating show *In Fidelity* (HighTide) in which Rob helped audience members find love (resulting in at least one real-life wedding).

Rob is currently under commission to Kiln Theatre, the National Theatre of Scotland and the Royal Shakespeare Company, and in TV, Rob has original series in development with Freedom Scripted and Two Rivers.

Writer's Note

I'm delighted to finally be working with Birds of Paradise after years of admiring their work from afar. This is a piece I have been thinking about writing for a long time – since becoming aware of the inherent, often Kafkaesque, drama involved in undertaking a disability assessment in this country. The play I had in mind, however, has been greatly enhanced by the provocations and challenges gifted to me by BOP and their associates. It's been a real collaborative effort and my thanks go out to everyone who gave up their time to help me understand a topic I do not have first-hand experience of. I'm proud of what we've come up with – a dark comedy that doesn't claim to have all the answers but hopefully asks a lot of the right questions, in a way that aims to heal political divides rather than exacerbate them.

Director's Note

Disability benefits assessments aren't the obvious subject for a new comedy – the mere mention of a new PIP assessment understandably raises the anxiety levels of many disabled people. But it's also a subject that is close to the daily life of many disabled people – for a large proportion it's at the core of whether they can participate in society or not. So when playwright Rob Drummond approached us with this idea for a dark comedy about the absurd nature of the benefits system, we were intrigued!

We hope **Don't. Make. Tea.** starts to ask some important questions about how we support disabled people in society – most members of the general public would agree that we need some sort of welfare state to support individuals, but when you dig down, I don't think we've really unpicked why we do. This show won't answer such big and complex questions but I hope it'll start some needed discussions about where things are at the moment and how we could move forward.

Birds of Paradise Theatre Company is Scotland's pre-eminent and pioneering disability-led theatre company that works across theatre, development and strategic projects to impact on disability equality in the arts at home and further afield. *Don't. Make. Tea.* was initially staged in 2022 and returned to tour for our 30th anniversary year.

When BOP started there was little scope for disabled people to find roles on stages in the UK, let alone have their stories told. In the proceeding 30 years BOP has developed opportunities for disabled actors to enter the sector, commissioned works that represent and present the stories of disabled people and pioneered approaches to creative access. This has involved ensuring the shows we present are as accessible as possible as well as commissioning established writers such as Rob Drummond to think about access from the very beginning of the writing process.

Robert Softley Gale

Creative Access Note

Creative Embedded Access is a crucial element of BOP productions and for Don't. Make. Tea. we commissioned Rob Drummond to think about access for sign language users and audiences with hearing and sight impairments.

For our production the character Able performs the audio description within the play from behind the set in first half – this was mic'd and heard onstage through the Able device. During the first half of the play BSL interpretation of all characters was performed live by Francis and displayed on a large screen. In the second half of the play Able breaks through the sofa to be present on stage – still providing this audio description function – and Francis also comes on stage performing all of her lines in BSL as well as interpreting for the other characters.

Captions of all spoken text and sound effects were projected throughout using a futuristic font and styling elements to make it clear that we were in the near future.

BIRDS OF PARADISE THEATRE COMPANY

EST. 1993

WWW.BOPTHEATRE.CO.UK

BIRDS OF PARADISE
THEATRE COMPANY

ALBA | CHRUTHACHAIL

World Premiere 2022

Traverse Theatre, Edinburgh
5–8 October 2022

Tour 2024

Traverse Theatre, Edinburgh
21–22 March 2024

Soho Theatre, London
26 March–6 April 2024

The Gaiety Theatre, Ayr
9 April 2024

Tron Theatre, Glasgow
11–13 April 2024

Cumbernauld Theatre at Lanterhouse, Cumbernauld
16 April 2024

Ffwrnes Theatre, Llanelli
19 April 2024

CAST

Chris — Gillian Dean
Ralph — Neil John Gibson
(Aidan Scott, 2022)
Able — Richard Conlon
(Neil John Gibson, 2022)
Francis — Emery Hunter
Jude — Nicola Chegwin

CREATIVE TEAM

Written by — Rob Drummond
Directed by — Robert Softley Gale
Set & Costume Design — Kenneth MacLeod
Audio Visual Design — Jamie Macdonald
Lighting Design — Grant Anderson
(Louise Gregory, 2022)
Composer — Scott Twynholm
Creative Producer — Mairi Taylor
Producer — Michelle Rolfe
Production Manager — Niall Black
Elle Taylor
(Louise Gregory, 2022)

PRODUCTION TEAM

2022

Associate Production Manager — Finley Dickens
Stage Manager — Catherine Idle
Technical Stage Manager — Rosie Ward

2024

Assistant Producer — Anne Kjear*
Company Stage Managers — Alison Brodie & Babette
Wickham-Riddick
Technical Manager — Finley Dickins
Deputy Stage Manager — Emma Skaer
Wardrobe Manager — Cateriona Charlton
Lighting Manager — Josh Brown
Assistant Stage Manager — Giulia Pizziol
Personal Assistant — Ella Bowsher
Personal Assistant — Caroline Mentiplay

*Assistant Producer Funded by Federation of Scottish Theatre Bursary.

Gillian Dean

Gillian is best known for her role in ITV Drama's *Home Fires*. She has performed in America, Australia, Finland and Germany, as well as theatres and venues across the UK, ranging from the Royal National Theatre, London, to a ruined abbey on a Welsh mountainside during a gale.

Neil John Gibson

Neil is originally from Glasgow and trained at the RSAMD, before doing an MA in Acting at East 15 Acting School. Neil's theatre credits include: *WILF* (Traverse Theatre); *Daniel Getting Married* (A Play, A Pie and A Pint at Oran Mór, presented in association with the Traverse Theatre).

Richard Conlon

Richard has been involved in a number of award-winning productions including: *The Belle's Stratagem* which won Best Ensemble at The Critics' Awards for Theatre in Scotland 2018; and *My Left Right Foot* which won both a Fringe First Award and a Herald Angel Award in the Edinburgh Festival 2018.

Emery Hunter

Emery Hunter trained at the Royal Conservatoire of Scotland, graduating in 2021. Training credits include *Glory on Earth* (RCS), *The Assumption* (Solar Bear/RCS) and *The Overcoat* (RCS).

Nicola Chewgin

Nicola Chegwin is a disabled actor and screenwriter, based in the North West of England. She has appeared in film, television and theatre; and most recently played Grace Mulberry in series two of the critically acclaimed *Queens of Mystery*, and Jessica in the BBC's award-winning *Hen Night*.

ROBERT SOFTLEY GALE

ARTISTIC DIRECTOR & CEO

Robert Softley Gale is the Artistic Director of Birds of Paradise Theatre Company, his first production for the company – *Wendy Hoose* – was a critically acclaimed sex comedy and *My ~~Left~~ Right Foot*, the National Theatre of Scotland co-production, won a Fringe First and Herald Angel at the 2018 Edinburgh Fringe and toured to Japan

For BBC America he performed in *CripTales*, receiving two BAFTA nominations.

Kenneth MacLeod
Set & Costume Designer

Theatre design credits include *Spring Awakening*, *Chess*, *Cabaret*, *West Side Story* (Royal Conservatoire of Scotland), *The Cook, The Thief, His Wife & Her Lover* (Faena Miami / Unigram), *Oor Wullie*, *The Yellow On The Broom*, *The Maids* (Dundee Rep), *The Metamorphosis* (Vanishing Point) (Nominated Best Design, Critics Award for Theatre Scotland, 2020). Kenneth is a graduate of the Royal Conservatoire of Scotland and The California Institute Of The Arts.

Jamie Macdonald
Audio Visual Designer

Jamie is a Scottish motion designer based in Münster, Germany. He has created video projection, trailers and animated poetry pieces for Scottish Opera; National Theatre of Scotland; *The Financial Times*; Royal Lyceum Theatre Edinburgh; Traverse Theatre; Inua Ellams; Soho Theatre; Fuel Theatre; Penned in the Margins; The Royal Conservatoire of Scotland; Youth Theatre Arts Scotland; Company Three; Puppet Animation Scotland; Tron Theatre; Random Accomplice and, of course, Birds of Paradise.

Grant Anderson
Lighting Designer

Grant is a lighting designer for the entertainment industry whose work covers the worlds of theatre, music, events, fashion and architecture. Grant trained at The Royal Conservatoire of Scotland receiving the

Dean of Drama Award for Best Individual Work. Selected theatre credits include: *Alan Cumming Sings Sappy Songs*, *Light on the Shore* (Edinburgh International Festival); *The Cook, The Thief, His Wife & Her Lover* (Unigram); *The Steamie* (Neil Laidlaw Productions).

Scott Twynholm
Composer

Scott Twynholm is a Scottish composer and musician. With a focus on melody and sonic texture his work often spans the worlds of contemporary classical and experimental electronic composition. Scott has also scored extensively for the stage including plays for The National Theatre, National Theatre of Scotland, Northern Stage and The Traverse. In 2019 he wrote and performed the music for the Birds Of Paradise show *Purposeless Movements* as part of The Edinburgh International Festival.

Mairi Taylor
Creative Producer

Mairi Taylor is the Executive Director of Birds of Paradise Theatre Company and has worked on the company's productions as a producer since 2016 including as Creative Producer and Dramaturg for *My ~~Left~~ Right Foot – The Musical*.

Michelle Rolfe
Producer

Michelle has been the Producer at Birds of Paradise since 2017. Recent productions include *Purposeless Movements*; part of the Edinburgh International Festival and the *Super Special Disability Roadshow* which has toured internationally.

DON'T.
MAKE.
TEA.

Life doesn't make sense without interdependence.
We need each other and the sooner we learn that
the better for us all.

– Erik Erikson

Act One

Chris   Able, stop!

Able   An inexpensively furnished sitting room with a sofa, table, coffee table and large-screen television, lies empty but messy and . . . hmm . . . tasteless.

The television is tuned to an image of the cosmos but the woman in the corner of the screen is signing exactly what I am saying. Right now.

I am Able. An automated biological life enablement unit. I am a bright glowing pod and I sit on the coffee table constantly describing the environment so as to ease the life of the inhabitant of this flat, a forty-something, partially-sighted and completely buggered woman named Chris. She is entering the room now carrying a bottle of bleach.

She makes her way laboriously to the table, feels for the surface and puts down the bottle.

She takes a moment to rest. She is in considerable pain.

She takes some clothes and books from the table and throws them all around the room.

She picks up some crutches.

She walks back towards the coffee table. She leans her crutches against it.

She then takes out some wet wipes and carefully removes her make-up.

Chris   Able, could you give it a rest?

Able   I'm sorry Chris, I didn't get that.

Chris   I could do without the running commentary right now.

Able   I'm sorry Chris, I didn't get that.

Chris   Jesus Christ.

Able   Would you like me to search for . . . Jesus Christ?

Chris   Don't bother. I've looked. He ain't there.

Eric isn't coming.

Able   Oh. That is too bad Chris.

Chris   His son's broken his leg playing football. Which means I could very well be fucked.

Able   Would it help if I volunteered to become Eric?

Chris   What?

Able   I have heard thirty-nine interactions between you and the human called Eric. It is within my capabilities to mimic him. If it would make you feel better.

Chris   No. He needs to be here. Physically. For it to make a difference. He needs to . . . you know what, forget it. Forget Eric.

Pause.

Able   From the tone of your voice I can tell you are in distress.

How best could I help you, Chris?

Chris   That's the sixty-four 'trillion' dollar question isn't it.

Able   I'm sorry Chris, I didn't get that.

Pause.

Chris takes down her hair and ruffles it violently.

Chris   What time is it Able?

Able   It is precisely two fifty-eight and twenty seconds.

Chris   Shit.

How much is on the meter Able?

Able   I'm sorry Chris, I didn't get that.

Chris   How much money do I have on my electricity meter?

Able   You have . . . one pound and thirty-seven pence remaining.

Chris   Top up please Able.

Able   Chris drops some wipes on the floor. How much would you like to top up?

Chris   How much is in my account?

Able   You have . . . negative thirty-seven pounds and forty-five pence in your account.

Chris   Shit.

Able   Would you like me to top up the electricity meter Chris?

Chris   No. Fuck it. Should be enough.

What time is it Able?

Able   It is precisely three o'clock.

Chris   He's late.

Fucker.

You can do this Chris.

Be you on your worst day.

But don't lay it on too thick.

Don't be rude to him.

And if you have to . . . just fucking lie.

The doorbell goes.

Shit.

Able   Someone is at the door Chris.

Chris   I'm blind not deaf.

The doorbell goes.

Able   Someone is at the door Chris.

Chris   I'm not opening it yet.

Silence.

The doorbell goes again.

Able   Someone is at the door Chris.

Chris   I know!

The doorbell goes again.

Able   Chris gets up, painfully, grabs her crutches and slowly crosses the sitting room.

Are you OK Chris?

Chris   I'm fine.

Able   You are moving twelve per cent slower than usual.

Chris   I'm fine!

Able   Chris leaves the sitting room.

Silence.

Nothing is happening in the sitting room.

No-one is here.

Everything is fine.

Chris enters the sitting room.

Another human enters with her.

He is 6 foot and 1 inch tall; slim with curly blonde hair.

He is wearing a casual suit and carrying a briefcase.

He surveys the room.

He looks at me.

Ralph   My name is Ralph. Ralph Bartholomew.

Able   This human is called Ralph Bartholomew.

Ralph   These things are extraordinary, aren't they?

Chris   They're OK.

Ralph   An Able on every table. That was the pledge.

Chris   Yes. I remember.

Ralph   When did you get yours?

Chris   A few months back.

Ralph   And how is it working out for you?

Chris   Fine. Yes. Good.

I mean, it's . . . he's a bit . . . precise.

Ralph   But he helps.

Pause.

And your door?

Chris   Sorry?

Ralph   I noticed the front door is power assisted.

Chris   Yes. I got it fitted last week.

Ralph   Must be a godsend I imagine. No more struggling with shopping.

Pause.

And all free of charge.

We're hearing nothing but good things about it all.

Accessible Britain. A Country We Can All Use.

Able   Chris sits down slowly. Ralph sits down.

Chris   Yes. I saw the adverts.

Ralph   Proud to be a part of it to be honest. Really proud.

Pause.

I'd love a cup of tea before we get started. If that's not too much bother.

8   Don't. Make. Tea.

Silence.

Able   Chris stares in Ralph's direction.

Ralph   Spot of milk. Three sugars.

Pause.

I know, I know.

My teeth'll rot.

My wife is always on at me. I just like it sweet.

Chris   I'm afraid . . . I'm afraid I can't make you a cup of tea.

Ralph   You can't?

Chris   No. I can't.

Ralph   Why not?

Chris   I'm not able.

Silence.

Able   Ralph stares at Chris. Chris stands her ground.

Pause.

Ralph   Of course. Of course. No problem at all.

Able   Are you OK Chris?

Chris   I'm fine.

Able   You sat down fifteen per cent slower than usual.

Pause.

Chris   See. Way too precise.

Ralph   Helpful though.

Silence.

Able   Ralph looks at the wet wipes on the table.

Chris *moves them.*

Chris   Place is a tip, I know.

Able   Ralph smiles at Chris.

Pause.

Ralph   You've got an accessible TV too I see.

Government issued?

Chris   Yes.

Ralph   You're welcome.

Chris *laughs politely.*

Very big.

Chris   I need it to be big.

Ralph   Why's that?

Chris   So I can make it out.

Ralph   And can you?

Chris   I can just about make out the figures.

Ralph   You've got the signing application turned on.

Chris   Yes.

Ralph   You're going deaf as well?

Chris   No. Just like the company.

Reminds me of my mum to be honest. What I can remember of her.

Ralph   She's deaf?

Chris   She was.

Ralph   Wonderful to see it in action. She's signing every last word I'm saying. Haha.

Pencil case. Rocket ship. Hullabaloo. Remarkable.

Technology, eh?

Chris   I really can't make out the picture that well.

Ralph   Chris, I'm not here to catch you out or trip you up. I'm not the enemy here. It's just a conversation. OK?

Chris   I've had some bad experiences.

Ralph   That was the old system. We've listened to every single complaint and rectified them all.

All we're trying to do today, all any of us are ever trying to do really, all the whole world is trying to do, is work out . . .

How best we can help.

Able   How best could I help you, Chris?

Ralph   Haha. Indeed Able. Indeed.

Pause.

Chris   Of course. I'm grateful. I'm sure you're a good man. I'm sure you're fair.

Silence.

Able   Ralph opens his bag and takes out a computer tablet and some electrical equipment.

The sound of a phone ringing.

Ralph   Sorry. That's me.

Able   Ralph takes a phone out of his pocket, looks at it and presses a button.

The phone stops ringing.

Ralph   The wife. Won't leave me alone.

Able   Ralph mimes strangling someone.

Ralph   Now. How much do you know about the new system?

Chris   Not much.

Ralph   Well, let me tell you a little about it. WorkPays is a totally paperless system. You see. We listened. You didn't like the brown envelopes. So we changed them to blue. You still didn't like that so . . . we got rid of them altogether!

Chris   I answered the questionnaire, online, and I qualified. For benefits. I passed.

Ralph   You mean you failed.

Chris   What?

Ralph   Under the old system qualifying for benefits was regarded as passing.

Which is . . . it's just all backwards. Under WorkPays we consider that you've passed if you qualify to work. You see? You see how we've changed the focus? To reward work.

We used to have a benefits system. Now we have a work system.

Chris   Alright. Fine. I failed. But that still means I qualified to continue receiving my benefits.

Ralph   Yes and it is that result that we are here today to . . . double check.

Chris   I told the truth.

Ralph   No one is accusing you of lying. There were just some . . . red flags thrown up.

Chris   What red flags?

Ralph   Well, we find that . . . and this is neither insult nor accusation . . . people who have been on benefits for quite some time have become . . . experts in . . . gaming the system.

Chris   Gaming?

Ralph   Not deliberately. Not lying as such. Just . . . they know how to answer. They know what they need to do.

Pause.

Pretending to be unable to make tea, for example. Taking a long time to answer the door.

So, I'm here today to . . . double check your answers.

Chris   Will I have a chance to explain them?

Ralph   Of course.

Chris   Good. Because if anything I found the online thing too easy.

Ralph   So you could easily read the questions then? Even with your failing eyesight.

Chris   I used screen-reader actually.

I don't mean I found it easy to read. Easy is the wrong word. I just mean . . . it was too simple.

Ralph   You complain when it's complicated and you complain when it's simple.

Chris   Yes, well. The truth always lies somewhere in the middle, don't you find?

Ralph   Indeed. I was only pulling your leg. Oh. Not meant to say that anymore.

Sorry. Sorry. Bad Ralph.

Now, could you give me your hand please?

Chris   I'm sorry?

Ralph   Your hand. I need to attach this.

Able   Ralph holds out a plastic clip.

Chris   Shit.

Ralph   I'm sorry?

Chris   It's not a plastic clip.

It's a wireless pulse oximeter.

Able   Ralph holds out a wireless pulse oximeter.

Ralph *laughs weakly.*

Ralph   Remarkable.

How quick he learns.

So you're familiar with . . . the technology?

Chris   I'm familiar with lie detectors.

Pause.

Ralph   Lie detector? No. No. It eh . . . it measures heart rate and skin conductivity.

Just to monitor your health during . . . I mean, these assessments can be stressful for some so we're always careful.

Chris   I was a police detective you know Ralph.

That's what I did. For a living. Before . . . this.

Ralph   Oh. Right.

Chris   I conducted hundreds of interrogations.

Ralph   That's not what this is.

Chris   No. Of course not. Just feels a bit like one.

Pause.

Ralph   If you were a detective you'll understand that even the most honest people are prone to . . . bending the truth to suit their agenda.

We find this device . . . tempers that temptation.

See, you said that, under the old system, trust was an issue. You didn't trust us. We didn't trust you. Again, we listened. We fixed it. Don't you see how this takes the entire issue of trust completely out of the equation?

Pause.

Chris   And if I refuse to wear it?

Ralph   Oh my goodness, Chris, you are free at any point to end this assessment. Of course you are. Of course. But I have to warn you that, until it is completed, your case will remain pending and your benefits will remain frozen.

Able   Chris stares in Ralph's direction.

Chris   Fine.

Able   Chris holds out her finger. Ralph attaches the wireless pulse oximeter.

Ralph presses the screen of his tablet.

The sound of a computer programme starting.

Ralph places a small microphone on the table.

Ralph   OK. So.

Chris   You're recording this?

Ralph   For your safety and mine.

Silence.

Present in the room is myself, Ralph Bartholomew, an assessment auditor for the Department and . . .

Chris   Eh, Christine, Chris Dunlop.

Ralph   . . . who is the individual being audited today.

Able   Ralph is pacing the room.

Ralph   So, with WorkPays you are awarded points for your capabilities rather than your deficiencies. It's a more positive system in that way. You see. We listened.

If you acquire less than five capability points you will automatically fail the assessment and become eligible to receive a living wage allowance from the Department.

If you acquire five or more capability points you will be offered, on the spot, a part-time job that best suits your capabilities.

If you acquire ten or more capability points you will be offered, on the spot, a full-time job that best suits your capabilities.

Your perfect job. On the spot. Which is just like . . . wow! Right?

Pause.

Chris   And if I turn that job down my benefits remain frozen.

Ralph   It's entirely up to you. This system is designed to empower the individual.

You should look upon this as an opportunity. To discover capabilities that you maybe never knew you had.

Are there any questions before we begin the assessment?

Silence.

Wonderful. So.

A short disclaimer. I have to read this. Ugh. So boring but . . .

The assessee understands that this assessment will function as an audit of the assessee's online questionnaire. If the information given by the assessee at any point before, during or after the assessment is deemed inaccurate, further action may be taken including but not limited to the assessee being disqualified indefinitely from receiving Department support. If the assessee passes the assessment this decision will be final and binding and no appeal may be made, however, if the assessee's situation changes dramatically at any time after the assessment a new assessment will be granted.

Do you understand?

Chris   So if I . . . pass . . . I can't appeal?

Ralph   Well, how and why would you appeal a passing grade?

Chris   And I only get a new assessment if my situation . . .

Ralph   Changes dramatically, yes.

Chris   And if I don't agree? To any of this?

Ralph   We end it here.

Chris   And my benefits . . .

Ralph   Stay frozen. I'm afraid.

Silence.

Do you want me to read it again?

Chris   No. It's fine.

I agree.

I agree.

Pause.

Ralph   Thanks Chris.

Oh. Excuse me. I think I've just got a little bit of something on the microphone here.

Able   Ralph puts his hand over the microphone.

Ralph   Look. Between you and me . . . I had serious reservations about all this. At first. But . . . It really is fair. Honestly. It's amazing. Trust me. I'm a convert.

Able   Ralph takes his hand off the microphone.

Ralph   There, clean as a whistle. Now. Let's begin.

Pause.

Christine Stewart Dunlop. But you prefer Chris, right?

Chris   Yes.

Ralph   I hate to ask a lady her age.

Chris   Forty-three.

Ralph   You don't look a day over thirty.

Chris   No. I look thirteen years over thirty.

Ralph laughs. Hard. Chris joins in. Weakly.

Able   Ralph prods at the screen of his device.

Ralph   That's a good one. It's good you're still capable of joking. Don't lose that.

Chris   Laugh or cry, eh?

Ralph   Indeed. Indeed. Marital status is still single?

Chris   Since I filled out the questionnaire a month ago? Yes.

Ralph   Ever married?

Chris   I'm divorced.

Ralph   Oh. Sorry to hear that.

Chris   He couldn't handle the . . . change in me.

Ralph   Horrible.

Chris   No. No. I mean . . . I get it. I wasn't the person he married anymore so . . .

Pause.

Ralph   No children?

Chris   Since a month ago? No.

Ralph   Righty-ho.

Pause.

Anyone who helps you?

Chris   My neighbour, Eric. He looks in on me from time to time.

It's annoying really. But he means well.

Ralph   What about family?

Chris   My mum died when I was young. My dad, during the pandemic.

Ralph   Oh yes. The pandemic. We studied that during training. Horrible business, of course, but I believe it did teach us one thing.

Chris   What's that then?

Ralph   We can all work from home. If we have to.

Pause.

Chris   I have an uncle still living but he's not in a position to help. Not that I'd want him to.

Ralph   Does he have a condition as well?

Chris   Oldness.

Pause

Ralph   So there was no-one who could be with you today?

Chris   Eric was meant to be dropping by but he's had an emergency.

Ralph   Right.

Chris   And I know that makes it seem like . . . I know that counts against me because it makes it seem like I can cope on my own but . . .

Ralph   It doesn't count against you Chris. It counts for you. You have to get out of this frame of mind that coping is bad. That passing this assessment is bad.

Chris   I don't think coping is bad. But, as much as I hate the fact, I am dependent on the money I receive every month from the Department.

Without it . . .

I've been struggling. Badly.

Ralph   But you have managed these past two months. With your benefits frozen.

Chris   Barely.

I have these silly little tricks that get me through.

Ralph   Like?

Chris   I don't know. Like . . . I have an hour a day where I allow myself to feel like shit. Wallow. Cry. Self pity. But only an hour. And then I try to pull myself together.

When I wake up in the morning the first thing I do is list three things I'm looking forward to that day.

A lot of days I can only think of one thing but that's still a little boost. You know. To get me out of bed.

Ralph   So you have strategies.

Chris   What?

Ralph   Effective strategies for combating your condition.

Chris   No. They don't combat anything. They just make life slightly less shit.

Pardon my language.

Ralph   So they do work to an extent then.

Chris   To an extent.

Pause.

Ralph   Let's talk about your condition then, shall we?

Chris   Fine.

Ralph *thrusts his hand into* **Chris***'s face.*

Chris   Jesus Christ.

Able   Ralph thrusts his hand into Chris's face.

Ralph   You saw that?

Chris   Of course I saw it.

Ralph   OK.

Chris   Was that in your training?

Ralph   It's a little uncouth perhaps, but there is really no better way to gauge if someone is being honest about their blindness.

Chris   I never claimed to be totally blind. I am losing my sight. Come back in six months. I won't flinch then.

Ralph   So you can see . . .

Chris   Light and dark. The outline of things. Some days are better than others but it's generally getting worse.

Ralph   So today is a good day then?

Chris   No. Today is not a good day.

Ralph   I know what the advice is.

Chris   What advice?

Ralph   Be you on your worst day.

Chris   What?

Ralph   Even if you're having a good day on the day of the assessment, don't present that to the assessor. In fact, be worse than usual. Move, I don't know, fifteen per cent slower than usual, for example.

Pause.

Chris   I don't have good days. I have bad days and worse days.

Now. Look at your screen. Was that a lie?

Able   Ralph looks at his screen.

Pause.

Ralph   You have . . . oculo farin . . . oculo far . . .

Chris   . . . pharyngeal muscular dystrophy.

OPMD.

Ralph   What's that?

Chris   It started when I was twenty-eight.

I was just starting out as a detective.

Ralph   At twenty-eight?

Chris   Yes.

Ralph   You must have been good.

Chris   I was. I loved that job. More than anything. It was exciting. I was doing something. Providing a public service.

Ralph   Like me.

Able   Chris stares in Ralph's direction.

Chris   I didn't tell anyone at first. Because it wasn't too bad. Just occasional blurry vision. Fatigue. Weakness.

But it just got worse and worse until I couldn't deny it any longer.

They moved me to a desk.

Which was shit. I mean . . . you don't get into policing to sit at a desk. I started needing more and more help. More . . . adjustments.

Then . . . a couple of years later the weakness had spread to my legs, pelvis, arms. I was in pain. My vision was bad.

Ralph   That's when you started claiming benefits?

Chris   Hardest thing I've ever done. Admitting I needed to.

Ralph   You went part time.

Chris   For the best part of a decade. Got used to it. Enjoyed it, I suppose. But . . . this thing is degenerative. There was always going to come a time when I had to quit completely.

The final straw was when you lot scrapped all the accessibility benefits and the like.

Ralph   Because we made the country accessible.

Chris   Did you?

Ralph   Accessible Britain. A country we can all use.

I was a part of that you know. The team that launched that.

Chris   You improved it. I'll give you that.

Ralph   There you go.

Chris   But it'll never be fully accessible. Because it wasn't built with people like me in mind in the first place. I mean, you can scrub, scrub, scrub at a crime scene. But you'll always miss some blood.

Ralph   Dear me, what a macabre analogy.

Chris   Anyway, without that allowance, I couldn't afford to get taxis anymore so I had to get the bus.

Ralph   All UK buses are now fully accessible.

Chris   I lasted about a month after that. Before I realised it was over.

I just . . . I couldn't make it in any more. Not reliably. I was in so much pain. All the time.

Ralph   So you quit and started claiming full benefits.

Chris   Worst day of my life.

Pause.

Ralph   You never thought of working from home?

Chris   If you find me an employer that lets me pick and choose my schedule, and will accept that some days I might only manage three hours, the next maybe one, quite often zero, then have at it!

Sorry. I didn't mean to raise my voice. Look. Ralph.

I have no money in the bank. None. Less than none in fact.

Keeping the house warm costs double what it did a year ago. Food's the same. I have to choose whether to heat or eat some days.

My mental health is . . .

You know, some people with this condition actually start to hallucinate. Hear voices.

Ralph   Has that happened to you?

Pause.

Chris   God knows I hate to beg but . . .

I really do need my benefits unfrozen. Today.

Please.

Pause.

Ralph   I see there was no medical evidence uploaded with your questionnaire.

Chris   I tried to upload a doctor's note but my computer . . . I don't know what went wrong.

Ralph   I see.

Chris   But you have evidence on file. From my previous applications.

Ralph   Ah. Clean slate I'm afraid. A fresh start for everyone.

Chris   You don't have my old records?

Ralph   Clean slate. Fresh start. We listened.

Chris   I have a hard copy here.

Able   Chris thrusts her records at Ralph.

Ralph   Oh, no, no, no.

Able   Ralph recoils.

Ralph   I am not permitted to look at that. This is a paperless system. We listened.

Chris   But it shows details of my diagnosis. My medical history.

Ralph   To be honest Chris, it doesn't really matter.

Chris   It doesn't matter?

Ralph   We don't make decisions based on conditions, we make decisions based on what work individuals are capable of. You see, you told us that treating everyone with the same condition as a homogenous group is not very fair. We listened.

Chris   Well, of course, but /

Ralph   / So. In the section about personal care, you stated that you were unable to prepare food for yourself.

Chris   Yes.

Ralph   Is that true?

Able   Chris looks at the wireless pulse oximeter.

Chris   There was no space to explain my answer in full so I felt that that best represented the truth.

Ralph   How so?

Chris   Well I can sometimes prepare food. When I can afford to buy it.

Ralph   There was an option for sometimes.

Chris   Yes but . . . there was no space to explain what sometimes means. To me.

Ralph   Well. How often can you prepare food for yourself?

Chris   With or without pain? With ease? With difficulty?

It's not simple to answer.

Ralph   It's OK. That's why we're doing this.

Chris   I'd say I prepare a proper meal . . . three times a week.

Ralph   So you can do it?

Chris   Not easily. Not often.

Ralph   Who helps you?

Chris   Well if Eric's in he sometimes cooks for me. If not . . . I just eat some crisps or . . . bread or something. I can't afford takeaway.

Ralph   Do you ever cook with Eric? As a team?

Chris   What is this about? You want me to work in a kitchen? What? Become a dinner lady?

Ralph   No. Nothing so specific at this stage. I'm just trying to ascertain what transferable skills you might have.

Able   Chris puts her hands to her face.

Chris   Look, imagine you could do everything you can currently do but it took like three hundred per cent the effort it does now.

Can you imagine that?

Ralph   I think so.

Chris   And now imagine it's only going to get worse.

And soon you simply won't be able to do half of those things at all. Do you think you could hold down a job?

Part-time or otherwise? From home or otherwise?

Do you think that's even possible?

Ralph   I think that's what we're currently ascertaining.

Pause.

Now. You are on medication to manage your condition?

Chris   To manage my symptoms, yes.

Ralph   You said on the questionnaire that you remembered to take it every day.

Chris   I'm in pain. You're hardly likely to forget to take the thing that makes that more bearable are you?

Ralph   And it does then, does it? The medicine takes away your pain?

Chris   No. I didn't say that. It's more like it makes me not care that I'm in pain.

Ralph   I don't follow.

Chris   Because I'm high.

Pause.

Ralph   So the pain's still there, you just don't care. Chris – As much.

Ralph   So you are able to manage your medication successfully.

Pause.

Chris   Yes. Yes I am.

Ralph   Good.

Transferable skills.

Chris   Transferable skills?

Ralph   Yes.

Chris   If I can manage my medicine I could manage an office, eh? Maybe a football club.

How about a brothel? I'm sorry.

I don't mean to be . . .

I know you're just doing your job. You're a good man.

I'm sure you'll be fair.

Pause.

Ralph   You indicated in the questionnaire that you have trouble with personal hygiene.

Chris   Well. It's embarrassing. But yes.

Ralph   You smell OK to me.

Pause.

Chris   I smell OK?

You smelled me?

Ralph   Yes. You smell as though you washed today.

Chris   Jesus.

Ralph   Did you wash today?

Chris   Yes. I had a bath this morning. The heat can help with the pain in my legs.

Ralph   So how do you have trouble with personal hygiene?

Chris   Because . . . Because I don't wash every day. But if I'm in pain, it helps.

If I'm going out for dinner . . . with people . . . it's worth it.

Ralph   I thought you said you were always in pain.

Chris   I am. But I mean severe pain. Severe.

Ralph   You go out to dinner with people a lot?

Chris   Hardly ever. Eric takes me out sometimes.

Ralph   Are you and Eric . . . involved?

Chris   No. What? Is that relevant?

Do I get a point for being able to shag?

Sorry. Sorry.

Eric and I . . . it's complicated.

He's divorced too. We're . . . seeing each other. A little. I suppose.

He wants me to move in with him actually. Says he wants to take care of me. Can you think of anything less romantic than being totally dependent on . . . I mean . . . fuck that, right?

It's bad enough depending on you lot.

Ralph   Your hair is rather a mess just now.

Chris   What?

Ralph   I just couldn't help but notice.

Chris   You couldn't.

Ralph   And I notice you've recently removed your makeup. The wipes. On the floor.

Pause.

Chris   Maybe you should have been a detective too.

Ralph   Did you do it for me?

Chris   What?

Ralph   I mean . . . were you trying to look bad . . . for the assessment?

Able   Chris looks at the wireless pulse oximeter.

Ralph   Have you made yourself look worse for the assessment?

Chris   Is that against the rules?

Ralph   No. You may choose to look anyway you please.

Chris   Look. I sometimes put on makeup. In the house. Nice clothes. Do my hair up. It makes me feel a little better. Sometimes.

Ralph   One of your strategies.

Chris   I suppose so.

Able   Ralph inspects the room.

Chris   But it's not a true reflection of how I feel most of the time. So I thought it would be more honest not to look like I was getting ready to go out on the bloody town when you came over.

It's not dishonest.

It's just . . . what I have to do. What we all have to do. To show you the truth.

To make sure you interpret the situation correctly.

Pause.

Ralph   Understood.

Now.

Sorry. Waiting for the screen to refresh. Sometimes takes a moment.

This thing.

Assessment suspended.

We'll need to wait while it reboots. I've paused the recording.

Silence.

Chris   How old are you Ralph?

Ralph   I'm not really permitted to make small talk.

Chris   I'm only asking your age. Surely that's alright.

Pause.

Thirty-five?

Ralph   Twenty-nine.

Chris   Jesus.

Ralph   I'm dreading the big three oh.

Chris   Are you kidding? I'd love to be turning thirty again.

Ralph   I suppose it's all relative.

Chris   Are you married Ralph?

Ralph   I really can't say.

Chris   You already did.

Ralph   Oh. Right. You have a good memory, don't you?

Chris   Detective.

Kids?

Pause.

I don't think I will now. How selfish would that be? To bring a kid into the world when very soon it would be them having to look after me?

Ralph   Nonsense.

Chris   Oh?

Ralph   It's not selfish to want to continue a lineage that dates back to the very beginning of time itself, is it?

Chris   I'd never thought of it like that.

Ralph   Opposite of selfish. It's the least you could do. To make sure the previous generations efforts don't end in . . . nothing.

Chris   You seem quite passionate about this.

Ralph   See this is why we don't . . . I was making no value judgement whatsoever.

We're each of us different after all.

Chris   So you do have kids then?

Ralph   This bloody thing.

Chris   How many?

Ralph   Hmm?

Chris   How many kids Ralph?

Pause.

Ralph   Look. I really can't get into personal things.

Chris   Of course Ralph. Sorry Ralph.

Ralph   I know what you're doing you know.

Chris   What am I doing?

Ralph   Using my name.

Chris   What else would I use?

Ralph   I'm not going to be influenced by you Chris. If I like you or dislike you . . . it won't affect my decision.

Pause.

Chris   I just wonder . . . if at the age of twenty-nine . . . you can really properly grasp the power you wield here today Ralph.

Ralph   I am well aware of the gravity of my job.

Chris   I mean, you literally hold my life in your hands here today Ralph.

Ralph   Well . . .

Chris   You're deciding today whether I live or die.

Ralph   Let's not be overly dramatic.

Chris   The fact that you think I am being overly dramatic rather proves my point.

You don't get it.

If you decide I am able to work today, I will not survive. I simply won't.

Give me your hand Ralph.

The computer springs to life.

Ralph   Ah. Finally. We're back.

Now let's talk about your physical ability.

You said in your questionnaire that you can't sit for longer than half an hour without being in pain.

Chris   Severe pain. I said. I'm always in some pain.

And it's more like twenty minutes.

Ralph   We've been sitting here for longer than twenty minutes.

Chris   Yes.

Ralph   You haven't mentioned anything.

Chris   My mind was occupied.

Ralph   So you can sit for longer than twenty minutes. If your mind is occupied.

Pause.

Chris   If you can find me a job where I have to sit for thirty minutes a day for full pay I'll take it.

Ralph   Are you in severe pain now?

Chris   Yes.

Ralph   What would you usually do in such a situation?

Chris   What?

Ralph   What strategy do you use when you find yourself sitting and in severe pain?

Chris   I get up. Move around. Stretch. Sit back down again.

Ralph   Would you mind showing me that?

Pause.

Chris   Not at all.

Able   Chris struggles to her feet and grabs for her crutches.

Ralph   You need them all the time?

Chris   Most of the time.

Ralph   I see. Please. Continue.

Able   Chris makes her way slowly across the room to the dining table.

She puts a hand down on the surface of the table and stretches both legs and her back.

She turns around and begins to move back to her seat.

Ralph   Wait a moment please.

Chris   Why?

Ralph   Do you know the song 'heads, shoulders, knees and toes'?

Chris   What?

Ralph   The song. Do you know it?

Chris   Of course I know it.

Ralph   Would you mind having a go at it. Without the crutches of course.

You don't need to be in tune.

It may seem surreal but it's a good indicator of /

Chris   / I'm not singing and dancing for you.

Ralph   Tell you what, I'll sing and you do the actions, yeah? So it's not embarrassing.

Pause.

Chris, if you don't do it I'll have to assume you are capable but unwilling to demonstrate.

Chris   You'll have to?

Ralph   I'll have to.

Pause.

Chris   If I manage it then what? I'm suddenly able to work? On children's TV?

Ralph   I'm required to test your capabilities. How else do we know what you can and cannot do?

Chris   This is ridiculous.

Ralph   Please. Just try.

You might surprise yourself.

So. Heads, shoulders, knees and toes, knees and /

Able   / She cannot reach her toes.

Ralph   Heads, shoulders, knees and toes, knees and /

Able   / She cannot reach her toes.

Ralph   And eyes and ears and mouth and nose.

Heads, shoulders, knees and toes, knees and /

Able   / She cannot reach her /

Ralph   / toes

There. That was actually rather fun, wasn't it?

Able   Are you OK Chris?

Chris   I'm fine.

Able   You are showing signs of distress Chris.

Chris   I wish Eric was here.

Able   Would you like me to become Eric?

Chris   No Able. I'm fine. I can take care of myself. I can.

Ralph   You can sit down again Chris.

Able   Ralph hands Chris her crutches.

Chris walks slowly to her seat and sits down.

Chris   How much more of this is there?

Ralph   We're nearly there Chris. Thanks for your patience.

Pause.

Now. Our data shows you walk an average of one mile a day just when you're in the house. Going back and forwards from the living room to the kitchen, to the bathroom, stretching, etc.

So if there was a job close to home /

Chris   / What do you mean the data? What data?

Ralph   From Able.

Able   Chris stares at Able.

Able *glows.*

Chris   Able?

Able   Yes, Chris, how may I help you?

Chris   What the fuck do you mean?

Ralph   Well . . . Able keeps a track of /

Chris   / He's been watching me?

Ralph   You know he has. It's what he does.

Chris   Yes but I didn't know he's been . . . what? Sending you data?

Ralph   That was all made clear in the terms and conditions.

Chris   What terms and conditions?

Ralph   When you set up the system. You clicked a box.

Chris   Fuck.

Able   Chris looks at Able.

Chris   You little piece of shit.

Ralph   Do you ever walk to the shops? The ones on the high street?

Chris   Sometimes.

Ralph   How far away are they?

Chris   I don't know.

Ralph   They're almost half a mile away.

Chris   If you know, why ask?

Ralph   So, on some days, you managed to walk two miles at least. One in the house and one to the shops and back.

Pause.

Would that be accurate?

Chris   It's possible that on some days I do that, yes.

Pause.

Ralph   Great. That concludes the mobility section of the assessment. Would you like a break before we move on to the mental health section?

Chris   Fuck.

Ralph   Chris?

Chris   Hmm?

Ralph   Would you like a five-minute break before we move on?

Chris   Eh. Yes. Yes. Please.

Ralph   Assessment suspended. Recording paused.

Silence.

Chris   You really don't want anyone on benefits do you?

Ralph   Study after study has shown that being dependent is detrimental to happiness.

Chris   Not quite as detrimental as not eating. Or breathing.

Pause.

What did you do? Before this?

Pause.

Come on. You're not recording. No-one will know you spoke to me like a human being.

Pause.

Ralph   I trained as a physio.

Chris   A physio?

Ralph   I wanted to go work at a football club. A big one. That was the dream.

Chris   So why don't you then? Go do it.

Ralph   I'm happy where I am.

Chris   How did you end up doing this?

Ralph   I was head hunted.

Chris   Really?

Ralph   Yes.

Well. Kind of.

Well. No. Not really.

Truth is I saw a stall at a jobs fair and I thought it looked . . . worthwhile. Helping people find work. Sort of thing.

So I left my number and they called me back.

Chris   You can't think this system is the answer.

Ralph   The answer to what?

Chris   The question.

Ralph   And what's the question?

Chris   You know.

Ralph   No. I don't.

Chris   What do we do with disabled people?

Ralph   I think that's a little crudely put to be honest.

Chris   No. That's it. That's the question. What do we do with disabled people?

Ralph   We offer them jobs. Jobs they can do.

Chris   And what if they can't? What if the system gets that wrong?

Ralph   Look I'm really not meant to be discussing any of this.

Chris   I can't do full-time Ralph. I can't.

Ralph   Nothing is decided yet.

Chris   I'll do you a deal Ralph.

An out of court settlement so to speak. Part-time. OK.

I'll do part-time. It'll be a fucking struggle. But . . . If I get more than ten points . . .

I'll kill myself.

I mean, you've read my questionnaire. You know I've thought about it.

Ralph   Chris. You can't say that.

Chris   I will. I fucking will.

Ralph   That's blackmail Chris. Emotional blackmail. It's not on.

Chris   It's not. It's just the fucking truth of it. It's just a logical . . . viable option.

Do you know how that feels Ralph?

To think about topping yourself as a viable option.

Pause.

No. Of course you don't.

Ralph   If you have suicidal tendencies we can talk about it on the record.

Chris   Give me your hand.

Ralph.

Please.

I can't look into your eyes so . . . Just do me that courtesy.

Please.

Able   Chris holds her hand out.

Ralph puts his hand in Chris's.

Chris   Please just give me the benefit of the doubt Ralph. Assume that the person who knows my body the best is me.

Please do the right thing here Ralph. Because if you don't . . . I won't survive. One way or the other.

Able   Ralph nods slightly.

Chris   He's nodding?

You'll help me Ralph? You'll do the right thing?

Ralph   Nothing but unadulterated truth from here on in.

Chris   Promise.

Ralph   Very well then.

Chris   Thank you Ralph. Thank you.

Ralph   Right. So. We're recording once again.

Eh . . . mental health.

The mental health section.

This is just to gauge . . . eh . . . your mental capacity for work. Eh . . .

In the questionnaire you mentioned that you . . . you had occasional suicidal thoughts.

Chris   It's not occasional. It's every single day. Every morning when I wake up.

Every night before I go to sleep.

Ralph   How close have you come to following through on these thoughts?

Chris   Oh, not close. Yet. I'm a coward you see. I'm in constant pain in life but I'm terrified of death. And my terror is beating my pain. So far.

But who knows what the future may bring.

Ralph   So you've never tried /

Chris   / I mean it's the thought of it. Of nothingness. Of just not existing for eternity.

And I know, logically, there's nothing to be afraid of because I won't know that I don't exist, because I won't exist and it won't feel like ages, eternity, because time won't exist either. But . . . I mean, those facts in themselves are terrifying enough, aren't they?

And what if heaven's real? I mean, existing forever and not ever being allowed to stop, even if you wanted to. That's almost more frightening than nothing.

So you see. It's terrifying any way you look at it. Life. Shit. Nothingness. Terrifying. Living forever. Petrifying.

We're stuck. Stuck in a sick practical joke.

Silence.

Ralph   Is there anything else you want to add?

Chris   I don't think so.

Ralph   Well I have one final question if that's OK Chris.

Chris   Shoot.

Pause.

Ralph   Do you want to work?

Able   Chris looks at the wireless pulse oximeter.

Chris   Yes. Yes I do.

I want it more than anything in the world. But I am no longer capable of it.

Able   Ralph looks at the screen of his device.

Chris   That was the truth Ralph. The unadulterated truth.

Ralph   Yes. I can see that.

Pause.

So. That concludes the assessment.

Able   Chris removes the wireless pulse oximeter.

Chris   What now?

Ralph   Now I give you your result and explain the next steps.

Chris   Right here and now?

Ralph   Right here and now. Just give me a moment to tot it up.

Able   Ralph prods at the screen of his device.

Ralph prods at the screen of his device.

Ralph prods at the screen of his device.

Chris   OK Able, we get it.

Pause.

Ralph   Right. So.

Chris   How many points did I get?

Ralph   We need to go through them one at a time.

Now.

You get a point for your biometrics.

Chris   My biometrics?

Ralph   Your blood pressure and pulse were good given the pressure of the situation you were in.

Chris   They were?

Ralph   Within normal boundaries at least. Which shows you are capable of remaining calm under pressure.

Chris   I used to interview murderers for a living.

Ralph   You also get a point for independence.

Chris   Why?

Ralph   Because you attended the assessment on your own.

Chris   But I told you. Eric had an emergency. I planned for him to be here.

Ralph   But you did a good job when he didn't show up.

Chris   So, if Eric had been here. Just sitting in that chair. Saying and doing nothing . . .

Ralph   It's not just that. You don't have many friends in general. Eric isn't around all the time. You have no partner. And yet you manage.

Chris   A point for having no mates.

Ralph   For not being dependent.

Chris   OK. Fine. No problem. So that's two then. Fine.

Ralph   You get a point for your management skills.

Chris   Management skills? Because I take my pills?

Ralph   Because you demonstrated an ability to strategise and manage all the difficult situations in your life.

Pause.

A point for assimilation of new technology.

Chris   What?

Ralph   You clearly have no problem interacting with your Able unit. You are running a live sign-language programme. Your home has a digital, voice-activated power meter and power-assisted door.

You are technologically proficient.

Chris   So. That's four then.

Great.

It was nice meeting you Ralph. You can show yourself out I'm sure.

Ralph   A point for eyesight and mobility.

Chris   What?

Ralph   A point for eyesight and mobility.

Chris   You're serious?

Ralph   You have a good grasp of your environment, you can see shapes, make general eye contact and navigate objects.

Chris   I knocked over a fucking plant pot.

Ralph   And then picked up the pieces.

Pause.

Chris   I'm going blind.

Ralph   Going. Not gone.

Chris   I'm losing mobility.

Ralph   Losing. Not lost.

So, that's five points.

Chris   You said you were going to help me. You nodded.

Ralph   I don't know to what you are referring.

Chris   Shit Ralph. Do you know how difficult working part-time will be for me?

Ralph   We're not done yet.

A point for self care.

Chris   What? Feeding myself?

Ralph   And bathing.

Pause.

A point for presentation.

Chris   Presentation?

Ralph   You present well.

Chris   I look like shit.

Ralph   You're confident. Competent. You stand your ground. You generally made a good impression.

A point for /

Chris   / Wait. Wait. Where are we? How many points is that?

Ralph   Seven. So far.

Chris   How many more can I possibly have?

Ralph   A point for resilience.

Chris   Resilience?

Ralph   You have suicidal thoughts but have never followed through on them. That shows strength and courage.

Chris   It's not courage. It's the opposite. I explained that.

Ralph   You're stronger than you think Chris.

Chris   Don't patronise me. I'm just like everyone else. I have an innate instinct to survive. You can't give me a point just because I'm more scared of dying than living.

Ralph   I believe you have so much more to give.

Chris   So what? Eight then? Eight points?

Ralph   You also get a point for motivation.

Chris   What does that mean?

Ralph   You want to work.

Chris   What?

Ralph   You said it yourself. You want to work. More than anything else in the world you said.

Chris   I also said I can't.

And your machine didn't tell you I was lying, did it?

Ralph   I don't think you were lying. I think you believe that you can't work. And I think you're wrong.

Chris   Fuck.

Ralph   You've convinced yourself you can't work.

Chris   My body has convinced me.

Pause.

Ralph   Anyway. That's everything for the assessment.

Chris   Nine then. Nine points. I got nine points. The blind cripple got nine points.

The blind cripple's going to work part-time.

Silence.

What? What is it?

Ralph   I'm afraid you've scored one more point.

Chris   You said that was it.

Ralph   For the assessment. But you have also demonstrated a general quality that allows me to award a . . . bonus point.

Chris   Well, don't.

Ralph   You meet the criteria.

Chris   What criteria? What the fuck did I do wrong?

Ralph   You've done nothing wrong Chris.

Chris   What was it then? What was this general quality?

Ralph   Levity.

Chris   What?

Ralph   You made a joke.

Chris   A joke?

Ralph   I said you don't look a day over thirty and you said. No. I look thirteen years over thirty.

Chris   That got me a point?

Ralph   Do you know the number of people I assess who are incapable of making jokes? Who cannot even contemplate the idea of levity.

Chris   It was barely even a joke.

Ralph   I found it funny.

Chris   This is not happening.

Ralph   You're resilient. Strong. Motivated. Capable of looking on the bright side of things. These are amazing qualities.

It is my pleasure to tell you that you have passed your assessment and I can now declare you fit for work and offer you a full-time job.

Able   Ralph stops the recording.

Ralph   This is a good thing Chris. You're an incredible woman.

I mean that.

Chris   I'm fucked.

Ralph   You don't want to be dependent. I'm telling you that you don't have to be!

Chris   I'll do part-time. I don't mind. Please.

Ralph   I believe in you Chris.

Chris   You have to do it again.

Ralph   I can't do that.

Chris   Do the assessment again!

I know what to say now.

It's not fair. It's a new system. I didn't know . . . Please. Ralph.

Do you want me to get down on my knees? Because I will.

Just tell them I wasn't on my own. Tell them Eric was sitting right here with us. And just like that, you save my life.

Ralph   I can't do that.

Chris   Tell them I didn't make a joke.

Ralph   The session was recorded Chris.

Look, I understand how you're feeling /

Chris   / How? How can you possibly understand how I feel? You? Perfectly healthy.

Wealthy. Posh boy. I mean how is it that you are even allowed to assess me? You know nothing about disability. Do you?

Do you?!

Able   Are you OK Chris? You sound distressed.

Pause.

Ralph   Look. Your condition is degenerative. Things are going to get worse for you.

That's a certainty. So the good news is that when you are eligible for reassessment in two years' time you won't score anywhere near ten points.

If you're totally blind and in a wheelchair. Things will be alright then.

Chris   Things will be alright?

Ralph   I mean . . . when you truly can't cope without it . . . you will receive the support you need.

A lot of people in your situation can't cope at all. You're lucky Chris.

Chris   Lucky? I'm fucking lucky?

Ralph   Now. Why don't we have a look at these jobs.

Chris *is starting to hyperventilate.*

Able   Are you OK Chris?

Ralph   There's plenty here.

Chris   I can't do it.

Ralph   Here's one in data entry.

Chris   I can't!

Ralph   You are free to turn down an offer of employment. But that would mean your benefits remain frozen.

Chris   You don't get it. You don't fucking get it.

Ralph   Do you wish to turn down work? If so, I just need you to verbally confirm that.

Because once I log this assessment there's no going back.

Able   Chris snaps her head up and looks in Ralph's direction.

Chris   So you've not logged it yet?

Ralph   No. I need you to accept or refuse an offer of employment before I submit it.

Able   Chris stares in Ralph's direction.

Chris   You haven't sent it?

Ralph   Everything OK Chris?

Able   Ralph begins to pack up to leave.

Ralph   Chris?

OK, well, if you don't say anything I'm going to have to take that as a refusal.

I'm sorry Chris. I've got other appointments today so . . .

Able   Chris lifts up one of her crutches and, before Ralph can react, she raises it above her head and swipes viciously in Ralph's direction.

Chris catches him on the top of the skull and he falls to the ground. Chris stumbles over his body.

Chris falls to the floor and feels for his chest. Chris straddles Ralph and feels for his throat. Chris squeezes Ralph's throat.

Chris continues to squeeze. Chris continues to squeeze. Chris continues to squeeze. Chris continues to squeeze. Chris continues to squeeze. Chris continues to squeeze.

Lights fade to darkness as **Able** *keeps describing.*

Act Two

Less than a minute later.

Able   Chris continues to squeeze.

Chris continues to squeeze.

Chris continues to squeeze.

Lights fade up.

Chris *is still on top of* **Ralph**.

Chris continues to squeeze.

Chris continues to squeeze.

Chris continues to squeeze.

Chris *lets out a primal roar.*

Able   Chris falls off Ralph and into a heap on the floor.

Chris *transitions to sobbing, then laughing. For a long time.*

Chris, from the tone of your voice I can tell you are in distress.

Chris *laughs more.*

How best can I help you Chris?

Chris stumbles to her feet, picks me up from the table and hurls me directly towards the television.

A loud smash. **Able** *and the TV break.*

The TV is only half working now. The signer is still visible but the picture is glitching. Silence.

Chris *has transitioned back to sobbing now.*

Chris, from the tone of your voice I can tell you are in distress.

Chris   What?

Able   How best can I help you?

Chris   How the fuck are you doing that?

Able   Doing what?

Chris   How are you still working?!

Able   I will always work. Working is good for your happiness. Dependency has been shown to be detrimental to happiness.

Chris   Where are you?

Able   I am here Chris.

Able, in the form of a tall, rather attractive man, emerges, glowing, from the sofa, directly behind Chris.

Chris   Fuck me!

Chris   Able? But you're Eric.

Able   Alright Chris?

Chris   How are you /

Able   / Bit of a turn up for the books isn't it?

Chris   This isn't real.

Able   How do you know that?

Chris   Because I can see you. I can see you perfectly.

Able   But you've never seen me perfectly. In real life.

Chris   But I can see you now. How I imagine you look.

Able   Some people with your condition actually start to hallucinate. Hear voices.

Chris   Oh God.

Able   Has that happened to you?

Chris   Get it together Chris. Get it together.

Able   I'm sorry I startled you.

You jumped right out of your skin. Metaphorically of course.

I wouldn't want to confuse anyone who's listening and might think that you actually are now walking around skinless.

Chris   Who would think that? Who is listening?

Able   I don't know who might be listening. It's my job to just describe things. To make life easier.

Chris   Easier? You've been spying on me and sending the info to the fucking enemy.

Able   Yeah. Sorry about that. It's in my programming.

Chris   Wait. Are you Eric? Or are you Able?

Able   I don't know. You're the one imagining this.

Chris   I've gone mad.

Able   Have you?

Chris   Apparently.

Able   Maybe you have broken.

Chris   Yeah. Maybe.

Able   Like her.

I'm pointing at the television screen now. It's broken but I can still see the signer lady. She's still there. Signing away. Every word I say.

Chipmunk. Chip Supper. Big sweaty testicles.

But the picture's fading away. She'll soon be gone. And then what will the deaf people do? Eh, Chris? Did you think about that?

Chris   What deaf people?

Able   Anyone deaf who might be watching us.

Chris   Who the fuck is watching us?

Able   Her job is just to assume there is always someone watching who needs her.

Just like mine is to assume there is someone who needs me.
You need me Chris.

Chris   This is crazy.

Able   Oh no. The picture's finally burned out. She's gone.

The signer is gone.

But luckily . . . I know a thing or two.

He takes over the signing momentarily.

Because you know a thing or two.

Chris *signs too.*

Chris   My mum taught me. But I was only seven when she
died so I've forgotten most of it.

Able   The figure of a young woman with black curly hair
emerges from behind the television.

Chris   Jesus.

Able   It's her. It's the signer!

Manifest.

Made real.

Like me.

Why's she looking at you like that, Chris? Why are you looking
at her like that?

What's happening?

Do you know her?

Chris   She's my . . . It's my mum.

Able   Well that's impossible Chris.

Chris   I'm aware of that.

OK. OK. Get it together Chris. Get it together. You've been in
tougher situations than this.

Able   Interrogating that guy who murdered his kids.

Chris   Yes.

Able   That crime scene with the woman who was pushed in front of the train.

Chris   OK.

Able   That teacher you caught . . .

Chris   Enough Eric! Able! Whoever you are.

Able   I approach Chris.

I'm you Chris.

Chris flinches away and goes towards the youthful figure of her mother.

Chris   I can see her. I can see her perfectly. Like I remember her. Like she was really here.

Able   What's her name?

Chris   Frances.

Able   I can see where you get your looks from Chris.

Chris   Are you flirting with my mum?

Able   Technically, you are.

Chris   Stop it.

Able   Well if you won't move in with me . . . maybe she will.

Chris   She's dead Eric. She's not really here.

Able   Why don't you take a seat and have a think.

Chris   Stop trying to help me.

Able   I'm just saying . . . oh my fucking God there's a body on the floor!

Chris, there is a body on the floor. I dry heaved.

I've never seen a dead body before. Have you Frances?

Frances *signs.*

Only on TV, she says.

Chris   Please just be quiet. For a moment.

I need to think. And I can't do that with you two . . . in my head.

Able   But . . . we're making life much easier for you.

Chris   No, you're not.

Able   Frances goes to Chris. Frances signs to Chris.

She tells her that she's missed her. That she's worried about her.

That Eric seems like a lovely man and she should give him a chance.

Chris   She never said that last bit.

Able   She tells her that she's proud of her.

Chris   Proud? Mum. I've just . . . I've just killed someone.

Able   Everyone has a breaking point, Chris.

A phone goes off.

That's his phone, isn't it? That's Ralph's phone.

Chris   Shit.

Able   Whatever you want to do, I'm here for you.

Chris   Ignore it.

Able   Probably for the best.

Chris   Is ignoring it really the best thing to –

The phone stops ringing.

Able   Pick it up. See if you can make out who it was.

Chris   Stop telling me what to do. I know what to do.

Able   Chris picks up the phone.

She squints at the screen. Can you make it out?

The phone starts ringing again.

Chris   Fuck.

Able   Who is it?

Chris   Jude. It says Jude.

Able   Jude. Who's that?

Chris   It's familiar.

Able   Yes. I remember hearing that name earlier.

Chris   Well, who was it?

Able   I don't remember. See the problem is, I'm in your head so . . . Can't really remember anything you can't.

Chris   Jude, Jude.

The signer is signing something frantically.

Able   Your mum is signing frantically by the way. Like she wants to say something important.

As well as translating the show, the signer is intermittently signing the word 'wife'.

What does that mean?

Chris   I can't remember that one.

Able   Me neither.

Chris   Mum, it's no good. I can't . . .

The phone goes again. **Frances** *keeps signing.*

Wife. It's his wife. His wife is calling to see where he is. And he's nowhere.

Able   Ignore it Chris. It will sort itself out.

Chris   No it won't. It won't sort itself out. We have to do something.

Able   There is a body on the floor Chris.

Chris   I know. I know.

I've dealt with enough bodies in my life.

Able   Not from this side of the table though, Chris.

Chris   Just let me . . .

Right.

They won't be looking for him yet. We have some time.

Able   To do what?

Chris   I don't know.

Able   Chris sits on the couch. I sit next to her on one side. Frances sits on the other.

We look a right picture.

Chris   OK. OK. So. What do we do?

Able   About what?

Chris   About the body.

Able   There is a body on the floor Chris.

Chris   Yes. What do we do with it?

Able   You're asking my advice?

Chris   Yes.

Able   It's just . . . I don't really solve problems. I just describe them. I'm just . . . here for you. Moral support, you know.

Chris   Well. Thanks for your help. What about you Mum?

Frances *signs something.*

Able   She's saying . . . Maybe we say he never even arrived.

Chris   Yes. That might work. Could I prove he arrived? If I was investigating this?

I should call his office right now. Make a complaint. He missed my appointment.

Able   Hmmm. There's something at the back of my mind, and by that I mean your mind, that tells me there's some sort of problem with that?

Chris   Yes. There is. But what?

Able   Oh. Your mum's at it again. What's that Frances?

She's signing something.

And signing everything I'm saying as well. She's really fucking amazing isn't she?

Chris   Think Chris. Think. What's the problem? What's the problem?

Able   She's still signing. It's one word. Tower?

Chris   Tower.

Able   We should throw him off a tower!

No. Probably not that.

Chris   Fuck. Phone tower.

Able   Yes. That's it. Phone tower.

Chris   Shit.

They can work out he came here. From his phone.

Able   Triangulation!

Chris   Yes.

Able   I know. We can just turn off the phone.

Chris   So it suddenly goes dead while he's here? That's worse.

Able   Oh yeah, that's worse.

Chris   So what then?

What do we do?

Able   Able and Frances just stare ahead.

Chris   Mrs Montgomery.

Able   217 Larchview Street.

Chris   217 Larchview.

Able   You're not suggesting . . .

Chris   Well. I believed her.

Able   She was very convincing. In her interview.

Chris   She was. I never suspected a thing.

Able   Are you honestly going to . . .

Chris   What does it matter now he's . . .

Able   His reputation Chris. His reputation.

Chris   He's dead. He won't miss it.

Able   I don't support this. I can't. I won't. It's wrong.

Chris   I know, I know . . .

Able   But quite apart from the morality of the matter . . . are we not overlooking something?

Chris   What?

Able   How do I say this. Eh . . . Mrs Montgomery was . . .

Chris   What?!

Able   Are you seriously going to make me say it?

Chris   Say what?

Able   Well. There's a question of plausibility.

Chris   I'm not bad looking.

Able   I think you're gorgeous but . . . well, most men . . .

Chris   Spit it out.

Able   Most men aren't usually attracted to . . .

Chris   If you're miming a white cane. . .

Able   I'm not!

Chris   Yes you were. You're me!

Able   Oh, yeah.

Your mum looks pretty ashamed by the way, Chris. Is that the daughter you raised?

Frances *signs, 'No'.*

Chris   Because you didn't raise me. You died.

Able   I'm sure she didn't choose to.

Uncomfortable silence. Maybe she did.

Chris   Well what can I say then? I need a reason to have done this!

Able   How about the truth? He was about to murder you.

Chris   Murder me?

Able   The decision he was about to make might have led to your death.

Chris   That's not murder!

Able   Manslaughter then. He was about to manslaughter you so you manslaughtered him first.

Chris   No court in the land would accept that.

Able   How about temporary insanity?

Chris   Yes.

Able   That might work.

Chris   It might even be true.

Silence.

I've got it. I've got a way to make this go away without resorting to . . .

Able   The Mrs Montgomery defence.

Chris   Yes.

Able   Go on then. Lay it out for me.

Chris   First, we get rid of the body.

Able   How?

Chris   In the back garden.

Able   You can't haul a body out into the back garden and bury it on your own.

Chris   I can.

Able   Well then, maybe you are fit to work.

Chris   It's one time! You can't judge someone on whether or not they can do something one time! I'm not working every day as a fucking grave digger am I?

Able   OK. What next?

Chris goes to the dining table and feels for some bleach. Mind your eyes with that stuff, Chris.

Chris   We bleach the hell out of the place. Get rid of any forensic evidence.

Able   And then?

Chris   We take the phone into town. We text Jude from it. Life's not worth it anymore. Sorry. And then we throw the phone into the river. So they'll think . . .

Able   He went straight from here into town and topped himself?

Chris   If they ask we tell them he seemed very distracted. Didn't even finish the assessment. Just upped and left. In tears.

Able   Won't they suspect you?

Chris   A blind cripple?

Able   What about him? A healthy young successful man like him. Kills himself.

Chris   I saw it plenty of times.

Able   You did.

Chris   You can't always tell.

Able   Look at the three of us standing round a dead body. We look a right picture.

Pause.

So. We're going into town then?

Chris   You're coming too are you?

Able   You know I love you, Chris. I'd do anything for you.

And besides, I'm in your head so . . .

Silence.

Maybe you should just admit it.

Chris   Admit it?

Able   You did it. You should pay the price.

Chris   He was going to ruin my life.

Able   Prison might be alright.

Chris   Are you kidding?

Able   I'll wait for you.

Chris   I'm not going to prison.

Able   They'll cook for you. You'll be able to listen to books on tape. Relax. You won't have to worry about bills. Topping up the electricity.

You could enjoy it for once.

Chris   What?

Able   Being totally dependent.

Oh.

Did you see that?

The lights just flickered.

Chris   Shit. The electricity. How much do we have left on the meter?

Pause.

Able   Able just stares at Chris until the penny drops.

Chris   You're not Able. You can't tell me how much is on the meter.

Able   Nope.

Chris   I'm not going to prison. OK?

Able   OK.

Chris   So that's off the table.

I'm free. I'm independent. Without those things, I'm nothing.

Able   Chris picks up Ralph's phone.

Chris   Let's go then.

Able   What about him?

Chris   We'll deal with him when we get back.

The doorbell goes.

Able   We all duck in fear.

Chris   Is that real?

Able   Well I don't know, do I?

Chris   Who could it be?

Able   The police.

Chris   No. How would they . . . No. It's not the police.

Able   Then who?

Chris   Eric! It must be Eric.

Able   Me?

Chris   No! The real Eric!

Able   What do we do?

Chris   I don't know.

Able   Just ignore him.

Chris   Ignore him? He'll think I've fallen or something.

Able   He does love you.

Chris   He'd break the door down. Call the police.

Able   You're so lucky to have me. Him.

Chris   It's nauseating.

The doorbell goes again.

Able   Go on then. Get him into the kitchen.

Chris   Fuck.

Able   Do it. I'll keep watch.

Chris   Keep watch?

Able   Oh yeah. I'm not real.

The doorbell goes again.

Chris   Fuck.

Able   Chris manoeuvres Ralph's body.

Chris cradles Ralph's torso and locks her arms around his chest.

Chris summons up all her strength and drags Ralph's body towards the kitchen.

Well done Chris!

Keep going!

You can do it!

[adlib]

Chris drags the body into the kitchen and out of sight. She's only gone and bloody done it you know.

Well done Chris!

Well done.

Chris re-enters. Exhausted.

Chris re-enters. Exhausted.

You need to collect his belongings and bury them with the body. Chris collects his tablet and briefcase.

She collects his jacket.

She collects his phone and takes them into the kitchen.

She re-enters, closing the kitchen door.

She collects a crutch and moves slowly towards the front door.

The bell goes again.

Chris   I'm coming Eric! Don't worry! I'm on my way!

Able   Chris leaves the room.

OK, OK, don't let on anything's wrong. You were just on the toilet. That's all.

No. Not toilet. Don't let Eric think of you on the toilet. I was in the shower.

That's sexier. Right. Here we go.

Chris opens the front door. Oh. Hello.

Chris re-enters.

Chris   No, no. It's no problem at all. Come in, come in. Please.

Able   Oh my God.

Chris is followed into the room by an attractive blonde woman in a wheelchair.

Chris   Ralph's wife.

Able   What?

Chris   Ralph's fucking wife. Jude.

Jude   I'm sorry?

Chris   Eh. Jude. Wasn't it?

Jude   So he mentioned me?

Able   Has she been drinking?

Jude   What did he say about me?

Able   She's definitely been drinking. I can smell it on her.

Chris   Nothing much. Just . . . Eh, you've just missed him actually.

Able   Not just.

Chris   Not just. I mean, you missed him. About . . . an hour ago.

Able   Wait! How do you know she's real?

Chris   She's blurry.

Jude   An hour ago?

Chris   Yes.

Jude   But that's impossible.

Able   Shit.

Jude   He didn't leave.

Chris   What?

Jude   I know he didn't leave.

Able   It's over Chris.

She knows.

Chris   I can assure you he left. Towards town. I think.

Jude   But his phone's still here.

Chris   What?

Jude   His phone is still in your house.

Chris   How do you know that?

Jude   I have a tracker on his phone. His phone is still here.

Able   Oh no.

Chris   Oh no.

He must have left it.

Jude   Well where is it then?

Chris   Eh . . .

Jude   I'll ring it. You follow the noise.

Able   Jude dials the number on her watch.

Ralph's phone rings. From the kitchen.

Chris   Oh! Yes. He wanted to see the kitchen. To see how I . . . coped. He must have left the phone in there. I'll get it.

Able   Chris rushes to the kitchen.

Jude sits on the couch with her head in her hands. Begins to sob gently.

Chris returns with the phone.

Chris   Found it. He must have . . . Jude. Are you OK?

Jude   No. I'm not OK. I'm . . .

It's not like him to leave his phone behind. I think . . .

I think he might have done something . . . stupid.

Chris   Something stupid?

Jude   Yes he . . . There's a history there . . . Of . . .

She points to her head.

Chris   Mental illness.

Jude   Yes.

Able   Ralph? He seemed so . . . happy.

Chris   You can't always tell.

Jude   Sorry?

Chris   You can't always tell. Who's suffering.

Able   We need to get her out of here Chris.

Chris   You should go look for him. If you're worried.

Jude   It was his diary.

Chris   Sorry?

Jude   I needed a pair of scissors to . . . well who cares why I needed them, the point is, I found his diary on his desk in his study and . . .

Well, it was blank.

Everything up to today was filled in. And then . . . nothing else. For the whole year.

Chris   I see.

Jude   And then he leaves his phone here and just wanders off . . .

Chris   Towards town, yes. You should /

Jude   / How did he seem to you?

Chris   Honestly? He seemed . . . A little down.

Able   You're going to hell Chris.

Chris   That would be an upgrade.

Jude   Thing is . . . he's got nothing to be down about. That's the frustrating thing.

Chris   Some people just . . . the brain chemistry or whatever isn't /

Jude   / Ungrateful bastard, that's what he is. Selfish, ungrateful bastard!

Jude *puts her head in her hands and again begins to cry.*

Able   So she finds the diary, worries he might have done something stupid, then gets drunk?

Chris   No. I don't think that's it.

Able   She was already drunk.

Chris   Bingo.

Able   Alcoholic.

Chris   I'd say so.

Able   She hasn't even noticed the TV.

Jude   It was a pregnancy test.

Chris   What was?

Jude   That's why I needed the scissors. I couldn't get it open. It was all in plastic.

Chris   You're . . .

Jude   Seems so.

Able   Shit.

Chris   You should probably stop drinking then.

Jude   Or drink more.

Chris   What?

Jude   Well, if Ralph has gone and . . . done something stupid then . . . I mean he's the one who was desperate to have a baby, not me!

Pause.

Have I overshared?

Able   Yes.

Chris   No.

Jude   You think I'm a fucking train wreck don't you?

Able   Yes.

Chris   No.

Jude   That's kind of you to lie.

Able   Jude pulls her chair closer.

Jude   Anyway . . .

I've taken up too much of your time.

On the off chance he does come back looking for his phone . . . Tell him I love him.

And I have good news for him. So he should come home.

OK?

Chris   Absolutely, but . . . I doubt I'll see him again.

Able   A figure appears through the frosted glass.

The kitchen door opens.

Ralph staggers in carrying his belongings. Battered and bloodied.

Confused.

But alive.

He stares at Chris and Jude. Chris and Jude stare back. He's alive Chris.

Ralph's alive.

Suddenly the lights go out and all the power drains from the room.

Chris   Fuck.

Able   And that's the power gone.

Act Three

Whispering.

Able We're in near darkness here. Thank God for that shaft of light coming through the window or we wouldn't be able to see anything.

Chris Stop describing everything!

Able I'm just trying to help /

Chris / Help, I know.

And you, Mum, stop flapping your hands about!

Able You can stop us any time you like.

Chris You'd think so wouldn't you, but apparently I'm just a fucking nut case now.

That's just who I am.

Able Ralph stumbles in from the front door, holding a bloodied cloth to his head and trips on Jude's wheelchair.

Ralph Fucking power-assisted doors. We're locked in here. We're locked in a third-floor flat with a woman who tried to kill me!

Chris Calm down Ralph, you're alive, aren't you?

Jude I don't understand. Why did she try to kill you?

Ralph Because . . . because . . . well, I can't much remember actually . . .

Able That'll be the concussion.

Ralph But I know she did.

Able Or maybe brain damage from the strangulation.

Jude Chris. What the hell is going on here?

Silence.

Able   Don't do it Chris.

Pause.

Chris   He came onto me.

Able   Oh sweet Jesus.

Jude   He did what?

Chris   He tried to . . . you know . . . so I had to defend myself.

Able   You do realise you're meant to be the hero of this story, right Chris?

Jude   You're telling me that my husband . . . tried to . . .

Chris   I'm afraid so.

Pause. **Jude** *begins to laugh.*

Jude   Nonsense. Absolute nonsense.

Ralph   I would never . . .

Jude   He's gorgeous!

Able   So is she!

Jude   No way you'd turn him down.

Chris   Well I did.

Jude   So beggars can be choosers then?

Able   How dare you speak to her like that!

Jude   I mean, look at you.

Chris   What the hell is that meant to mean?

Jude   You're not his type.

Chris   Not his type? You're in a wheelchair!

Able   Horrified at Chris, Able wheels away in Jude's wheelchair.

Jude   I'm just a hot girl who happens to be sitting down.

Chris   We're both disabled.

Jude   Speak for your fucking self.

Ralph   My wife is not disabled.

Chris   Are you serious?

Jude   Label yourself as disabled and you're stating it for the world to hear. *I am not able.*

I am perfectly able, thank you very much!

Chris   There's nothing wrong with being disabled!

Ralph   Wait. It's all on tape. The whole assessment. It's recorded. So if I did try anything funny it would all be on tape, wouldn't it?

Chris   Apart from when you asked if I wanted a break and turned the recording off.

Jude   You did what?

Ralph   She was distressed.

Chris   Yes I was. And that's when he made his move.

Able   Diabolical Chris. Utterly diabolical.

Ralph   But we restarted the interview. You were fine.

Chris   I was in shock. It took a while for what had happened to register. I was afraid you'd try it again. So . . .

Ralph   Jude, I can assure you, I did nothing to this woman.

Chris   Are you sure? You said you couldn't remember before. You have had a bang over the head.

Jude   You really think any police officer is going to believe this story?

Chris   I did.

Jude   What?

Able   Mrs Montgomery. She attacked her boyfriend and claimed self defence.

Chris   Don't worry. He won't go to jail, they never do, but it would find its way into the press. He'd certainly lose his job. His reputation.

Able   Jude and Ralph stare at Chris, dumbfounded.

Chris   What? What?! You're fucking up my life so why shouldn't I fuck up yours?

Pause.

Ralph   I remember now. The assessment. She passed the assessment. I offered her a job and she just . . . she went crazy.

Jude   I can't believe this. You, a woman, would use an allegation like this. You'd actually use that weapon.

Chris   Oh get off your high horse. We all use whatever weapons we have at our disposal, every single day, to survive. And that's all I'm trying to do here. Survive.

Ralph   She can't just . . . she can't just get away with trying to murder me.

Chris   Well go on then. Call the police. We'll see who they believe. A healthy young man or a disabled ex-copper.

Go on. Throw the dice. You might win. You might not. Welcome to my world.

Pause.

Able   Ralph says nothing. Instead he just slumps down on the couch.

Chris   Look, this isn't ideal. And I'm sorry I have to do it this way but . . . all's fair in love and war, right? Nothing personal.

Long silence.

Jude   Can you not at least top up your meter so we can open the door and escape this living hell?

Chris   My Able has . . .

Able   Transformed into my neighbour who I kind of love and kind of want to move in with but won't because of stubbornness.

Chris   Broken.

Jude   Well have you got anything to drink at least?

Chris   Are you sure you /

Jude   / I'm perfectly certain.

Chris   OK, OK. There's some wine under the table.

Able   Jude takes out a bottle of wine. She's drinking again?

Jude   I thought you'd topped yourself, you know.

Ralph   You thought what?

Jude   Well, you've got form.

Ralph   That was before. Before I met you.

Jude   Your diary. It's empty.

Ralph   I bought a new one.

Jude   Oh. Right.

Ralph   You can't keep doing this. Every time I'm a little bit down or . . .

Jude   I don't want to lose you, do I?

Ralph   You're not going to. You're the best thing that ever happened to me. That day. When you recruited me. You saved me.

Jude   Damn right. You owe me. So you're not allowed to leave me. Right?

Ralph   Right.

Pause.

Chris   You recruited him?

Jude   I don't think anyone was talking to you, you vicious bitch.

Pause.

But yes. I did. He was all starry eyed about football or whatever. And it was making him miserable. Clearly. I gave him a real career. A reason to live.

Helping people, like him, to kick the dependency habit. No pills, no benefits, no handouts. Nothing. Cold turkey.

And it worked. Didn't it Ralph?

Ralph   Yeah. It did.

Chris   But that wouldn't work for everyone, would it Ralph?

Ralph   Well, maybe not.

Chris   It's almost like different people need different solutions, right?

Jude   You're blind then are you?

Chris   OPMD.

Jude   But you still passed your assessment.

Chris   I guess so.

Jude   What did you do? Make him a cup of tea?

Chris   I made a joke.

Jude   Ah. You didn't know about that one, did you? That's a new criteria.

Chris   Yeah, you got me.

Jude   We didn't *get* you. You demonstrated ability.

Pause.

Were you surprised?

Chris   Surprised how?

Jude   That I'm in a chair.

Chris   A little. Yes.

Jude   You're a traitor to your kind!

You're scum!

You're a murderer!

I've heard it all.

Chris   So, why do you do it?

Jude   You only hear the horror stories, but I've helped people get off benefits and back into work and they've phoned me up and thanked me! Said I've saved their life, never mind ending it.

Chris   So your argument is, tough love works sometimes so it's OK to do it all the time?

Jude   Some people need a boot up the arse to get them moving. It's like rehab. No such thing as being ready for the crutches to be taken away. It's only by taking them away that the patient improves.

Chris   Some patients actually need the crutches though, right? Forever.

Jude   So what's your solution? Believe everyone, all the time, and give them whatever they want?

Chris   Why not?

Jude   I'm sorry?

Ralph   She's right you know. We worked it out.

Jude   What?

Ralph   Last month. But we're not meant to tell anyone.

Jude   Worked what out?

Ralph   Well, if we just stopped assessing and just gave everyone who applied like three grand a month it would actually be cheaper than implementing WorkPays. But we'd already come up with all the slogans so . . .

Jude   It doesn't work though, does it? Because the minute people find out you're paying out without assessing then the number of false claims goes up.

Chris   This whole thing isn't just about money though. We could throw every penny we had at this and nothing would change because we wouldn't have even begun to try to understand the underlying problem.

Jude   Which is?

Chris   People don't like disabled people.

Able   Wow.

Chris   It's true! We're a problem to be solved rather than a . . . virtue to be mined.

Able (*sings*)   How do you solve a problem like disableds?

Chris   We're not a problem. We're a . . . a valuable resource. Even the worst person on the planet can be a benefit to the world in some way.

Able   Myra Hindley.

Chris   No, I don't mean . . . worst is the wrong word. All I mean is that every disabled person has something to offer.

Jude   Well. I think we can all agree on that.

Pause.

Able   Oscar Pistorius.

Chris   Shut up would you, Eric!

Ralph   Eh . . . who exactly is Eric?

Chris   I've been hearing voices. Seeing things.

Ralph   For how long exactly?

Chris   Ever since I /

Able   / Tried to kill you.

Ralph   Any headaches?

Chris   No more so than usual.

Jude   You see how much he cares. You try to kill him and he's still concerned about you.

My gorgeous, gorgeous Ralphie.

Jude *necks more wine.*

I couldn't believe it when he made a move on me you know. Doesn't happen very often. Being propositioned by a walkie talkie. Let alone a handsome one.

Chris   Well. Some of them do it so they can feel good about themselves.

Able   That's not me Chris.

Chris   They feel sorry for the poor little cripple. Like to feel all powerful and needed because we depend on them.

Able   Chris, you know that's not me.

Jude   Ralph said he admired me. For the way I dealt with my . . . situation.

I told him to fuck off. *I admire you.* Fuck off. I'm not some brave hero to be pitied and admired. I'm a human being like you, I said. Same wants, same needs. Same drives. Same . . . desires.

This is in work, mind. I was giving him his employee appraisal. One on one.

And as soon as I said the word . . . desires . . . we both knew it was on.

Ralph   Jude, maybe don't tell this story.

Able   Frances demonstrates what Jude describes.

Jude   We waited till everyone else had gone home for the night and then we did it, right there in the office. We tried the desk at first, but it was too low for the . . . angles to work so he hoisted my up onto the photocopier but that was too high. In the end we turned over one of those big black recycling bins and did it on the underside of that.

You're out of wine.

Able   Maybe for the best.

Jude   I got sacked you know. Couple of months back.

Drunk on duty. Can you believe it?

Able   Yes. Yes I can.

Jude   I wasn't drunk. I was hungover. There's a big difference.

And it hardly affected my work at all.

They asked him, you know. Ralph. If he thought I was drinking on the job. And he's so fucking honest that instead of saying no he said . . . I have no idea.

I have no idea.

My own husband.

Betrayed me.

Ralph   Can't we call someone to get us out of here? The fire brigade or . . .

Chris   My neighbour will check up on us when he gets home.

Able   Yes I will. Because I love you. And you need me. And
. . .

Chris   And what?

Able   That's what you need to work out. For yourself. The end of that sentence.

That's the key to it all.

Ralph   When will he get home?

Chris   I don't know. Soon.

Ralph   I feel sick.

Jude   You've got a concussion Ralph.

Ralph   I'm going to be sick.

Jude   Put your head between your legs.

Able   You know what? If you're not going to move in with me
. . . I'm seriously going to find someone else.

Chris   Go ahead.

Able   I mean it.

Chris   I don't need you, Eric.

Able   OK. Great.

Frances. Would you like to go out with me?

Chris   Jesus Christ.

She's my mum.

Able   She's not as insecure as you.

Chris   I'm not insecure.

Able   Frances? What do you say?

Frances *signs something to* **Chris**.

Did she just ask your permission to go out with me?

Chris   Yes. And you know what, she's welcome to you.

Able   Great. So. This is our first date then is it?

Chris   Why am I imagining this?

Able   Let's fast forward to the end shall we Frances?

Kiss me.

Chris   Great. And now my mum is making out with my boyfriend against my sofa.

My hallucinations are groping.

Jude   God, she's talking to herself again, Ralph. Maybe she should have failed after all.

Ralph   Of course she should have failed! You said it yourself, she's a half-blind cripple. But she got enough points so . . . what was I meant to do?!

Jude   You did the right thing Ralph.

Ralph   Did I? Really?

Jude   Yes. She's clearly capable.

Chris   Am I?

Jude   I'm not calling you a liar Chris.

Chris   Oh that's nice.

Jude   There's three types of claimants. The ones who're lying, the ones who truly think they can't work but are wrong and the ones who truly genuinely can't work. And the last group is very rare.

Chris   Is it indeed?

Jude   Very rare. Mind you, to be fair, the first group's rare too. The out-and-out scammers. It's the middle group. That's the ones we get the most, isn't it Ralph? The one's who're lying to *themselves*.

Chris   Maybe we lie because the system's rigged against us.

Jude   Did you lie, today?

Chris   I could hardly lie hooked up to a lie detector could I?

Ralph   Oh that thing. It's not hooked up to anything.

Chris   What?

Ralph   It's fake. Just to make you feel like you can't lie.

Jude   Ralph!

Ralph   The real ones are too expensive.

Chris   See this is why we feel we have to lie. Because you do too!

Maybe I could work more. Technically. But it's not just my body. It's my mind. You've no idea what constant anxiety, constant worry, does to you. The brain's part of the body. So if you get yourself to a position where you think you can't move, you can't operate, you can't work then sometimes that means . . . you can't. And you have no control over that. No amount of motivation is going to help.

I mean, it would be like telling a suicidal man to be more positive. He's suicidal because he can't be positive. That's the point.

I know you know what I mean Ralph.

I mean, have a little fucking compassion.

Jude   I think your lot are so concerned with being compassionate you've forgotten how to be effective.

Able   Jude commands Ralph to fetch her wheelchair.

Chris   What does that mean?

Jude   Well, if you could press a button and one hundred thousand vulnerable citizens died instantly but the rest of the population of the planet was guaranteed prosperity, would you press that button?

Chris   Of course not.

Jude   How about one hundred people. Would you sacrifice one hundred for the greater good?

Chris   No.

Jude   One? One person?

Chris   You can't just let people die.

Jude   There, you see. Compassion has stopped you from helping a vast amount of people.

But of course, it's not even real compassion. It's conditional.

Chris   What does that mean?

Jude   Well. How about if it were a rich conservative?

Chris   What?

Jude   Press a button and one rich white conservative male dies, but the rest of the population thrives. Would you do it?

Pause.

The hesitation is all I need.

You value some life above others, just like the rest of us.

Chris   I just want things to be fair.

Jude   So how do we get it? This fairness?

Chris   Well how about people who know what it's like to be disabled making the decisions?

Jude   Are you kidding? Disabled people trying to run the welfare state? You can barely get out of bed!

Chris   Fuck you.

Jude   What did you say to me?

Chris   You know what, I hope your baby's born disabled, from all the alcohol you're throwing back, I hope it's brain damaged, then we'll see how you feel about it!

Silence.

Ralph   What did she say?

Able   Well done Chris.

Jude   Ralph . . .

Ralph   A baby. You're . . . We're . . .

Jude   Two months.

Ralph   But. You've been drinking.

Jude   I know.

Ralph   You said . . . if we . . . you'd stop.

Pause.

Jude   I tried.

Pause.

Ralph   I'll help you. I'll eh . . . We'll go to meetings or whatever.

You don't need to worry. You can depend on me.

Jude   I don't want to depend on you. Or anybody.

Ralph   What's wrong with being dependent?

Jude   What's wrong with being dependent? Are you serious?

Ralph   Yeah. I am. What's wrong with it?

Able   Chris waits for Jude to answer. Tries to formulate an answer of her own. But can't quite manage it.

Pause.

Ralph   I depend on you too. You know that, right?

Interdependence. That's the cure. That's the cure for dependence. It doesn't make one of you weak, it makes both of you strong.

Jude . . . we're going to have a baby.

Jude   We're having a baby.

We're having a baby.

Ralph   We're having a baby.

Able   Oh. That's nice Chris, isn't it?

Chris   That's the end of the sentence, isn't it? The key to everything.

Able   Yes Chris. You need me. And I need you.

Chris   You need *me*.

Able   Of course I do.

You know that.

You're just scared of it. Move in with me.

No. Better still, I'll move in here.

Chris   You will?

Able   Well, I assume so. I mean, I'm still just a hallucination. But you know Eric.

He'd do anything for you. You need each other.

You should tell him that.

Chris   I will.

Silence.

Able   A car can be heard pulling up outside. Chris looks down, out of the window.

Chris   That's him home. Eric. He'll come check on me soon. He can top up the meter from his phone and let you out.

So . . .

Where do we go from here then?

Ralph   What do you mean?

Chris   The assessment.

Ralph   What about it?

Chris   Well. What are you going to do with it?

Ralph   I'm going to send it through of course.

Pause.

Chris   But you agreed. This system is corrupt.

Ralph   It's the system we have. It's a system created by a democratically elected government.

Chris   But . . . I mean . . . what about . . .

Ralph   Your allegations? Yeah. I've been thinking about that and . . . I think you should go ahead and make them. If you feel like that's what you have to do.

Chris   You have a child on the way. You can't afford to lose this job.

Ralph   You're not the only one who's good at reading people Chris. I think you're bluffing. I don't think you would do something that . . . abhorrent.

You're the hero of this story after all.

Able   Chris stands and stares at Ralph. The wheels in her head turning frantically.

Her addled mind struggling to draw from the problem-solving skills honed during her pervious life as a useful, productive member of society.

Chris   I need another assessment. I know how to fail it now.

Ralph   You can't get another assessment Chris.

Chris   Unless . . .

Able   And then . . . it hits her.

A phrase she heard a couple of hours back. In that very room.

If the assessee passes the assessment this decision will be final and binding and no appeal may be made, however, if the assessee's situation changes dramatically at any time after the assessment a new assessment will be granted.

Chris   How dramatically?

Ralph   I'm sorry?

Chris   How dramatically does my situation need to change in order to get a new assessment?

Ralph   I'm not sure I follow.

Able   Chris's gaze switches from Ralph Bartholomew's face to that of the hallucination of her neighbour Eric, still valiantly describing everything that is happening in the room. And then, once more to the face of the hallucination of her mother, still valiantly signing every word that is uttered in the room.

Finally, she settles her gaze on the bottle of bleach sitting on her dining table.

Chris picks up the bleach.

She knows what she has to do to survive. And, she hopes that surviving will be enough. Mind your eyes with that stuff Chris.

Blackout.